Ice Breakers

Short Activities to Encourage Social Interaction

Concept: Geoffrey R. Lorenz
Author: Bonnie J. Krueger
Cover Design: J. Richards
Illustrations and Page Layout: Emily E. Myers

Printed in the United States of America

90/1026LE
ISBN: 978-1-4291-0404-3

BRIDGING the Gaps in Education™
Lorenz Educational Press
P.O. Box 802 • Dayton, OH 45401-0802

for other LEP products visit our website
www.LorenzEducationalPress.com

How To Use This Book

Ice Breakers is a collection of activities created to help build cooperation and teamwork within your classroom. Putting students together that may not know each other very well and encouraging them to get to know their classmates can strengthen interpersonal communication skills, classroom cooperation, and perhaps even spark a new friendship.

These activities are easy to organize and require few, if any, additional materials. Most of them can be played for multiple rounds to further increase their educational value. The reproducible game cards needed for some of the activities are included in the back of the book, and several of the games use the same set of cards. These cards can be reproduced on card stock and even laminated to reduce wear and tear; it will also save you the time of having to copy them again for future games.

National Standards

The games and activities in this book address the following National Education Standards:

Supports National Standards

English

- NL-ENG.K-12.4 Communication Skills;
- NL-ENG.K-12.5 Communication Strategies;
- NL-ENG.K-12.12 Applying Language Skills.

Fine Arts

- NA-T.K-4.2 Acting by Assuming Roles and Interacting in Improvisations;
- NA-D.K-4.2 Understanding Choreographic Principle, Processes, and Structures;
- NA-VA.K-4.3 Choosing and Evaluating a Range of Subject Matter, Symbols, and Ideas;
- NA-VA.K-4.5 Reflecting Upon and Assessing the Characteristics and Merits of Their Work and the Work of Others.

Math

- NM-PROB.PK-12.2 Solve Problems that Arise in Mathematics and in Other Contexts;
- NM-PROB.PK-12.3 Apply and Adapt a Variety of Appropriate Strategies to Solve Problems;
- NM-PROB.COMM.PK-12.1 Organize and Consolidate Their Mathematical Thinking through Communication;
- NM-PROB.COMM.PK-12.2 Communicate Their Mathematical Thinking Coherently and Clearly to Peers, Teachers, and Others;
- NM-NUM.PK-2.1 Understand Numbers, Ways of Representing Numbers, Relationships among Numbers, and Number Systems;
- NM-ALG.PK-2.3 Use Mathematical Models to Represent and Understand Quantitative Relationships;
- NM-GEO.PK-2.2 Specify Locations and Describe Spatial Relationships Using Coordinate Geometry and Other Representational Systems.

Social Sciences

- NSS-G.K-12.1 The World in Spatial Terms.

Table of Contents

Partner and Small Group Selection

Choosing partners or small groups for these activities is very important. Putting students together that would not normally associate with each other is a great way for them to get to know the other members of their class. Be sure to use a selection method that will combine students in a non-biased manner.

This method is sure to integrate your student groups and will let them have a little fun at the same time. Have the class line up according to any of these parameters:

1. *Alphabetical by last name*
2. *Alphabetical by first name*
3. *Birth date*
4. *Height*
5. *Alphabetical by the name of the street on which they live*
6. *Numerical order by street address*
7. *Numerical order by last four digits of phone number*
8. *Numbers drawn from a hat*

Feel free to choose your own criteria, but keep in mind that separating students by reasons such as gender or ethnicity could have a negative impact on the groups and should be avoided.

After the students are lined up according to the selected criteria, have each student count off in the number of desired groups. For example, if you would like the class to be divided into five groups, the first student in the row would say "One" aloud, followed by the second student with "Two," etc. After the fifth student says "Five," the counting starts over again with the next student saying "One." Continue counting until all students have a number. Students with the same number will make up a group.

Having the students discover their group members can be an ice-breaking activity in itself! For example, if you choose to divide the class based on birth dates, the students need to communicate with each other in order to find classmates with birthdays in the same month, and then arrange themselves in the correct order by the specific day before they count off into groups. This allows the students to get to know a little more about each other right from the start!

Games to Get Them Going

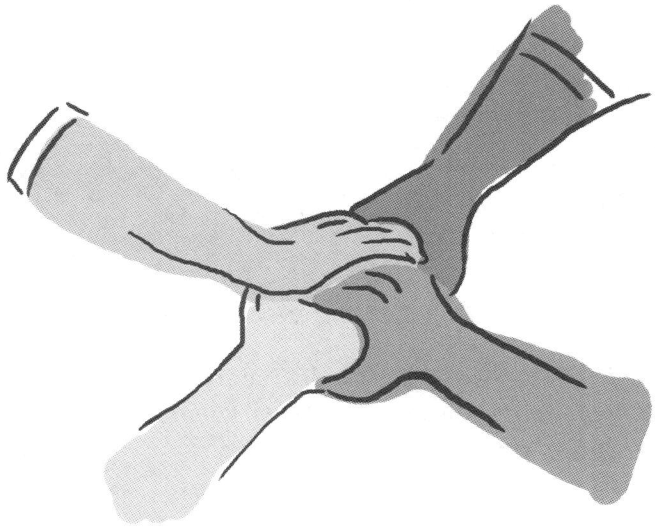

These quick and easy activities are sure to get your class excited about working together. Many of the games in this section will have your students up and moving around, while others provide them with a fun way to work while at their desks.

In many cases, it will be beneficial to the students to practice with the class as a whole before carrying out the activity. Make sure they feel comfortable with each activity to maximize its educational value.

Last One Standing

MATERIALS: Game Grid (page 43)
Paper clips, buttons, coins, or candies

DIRECTIONS:

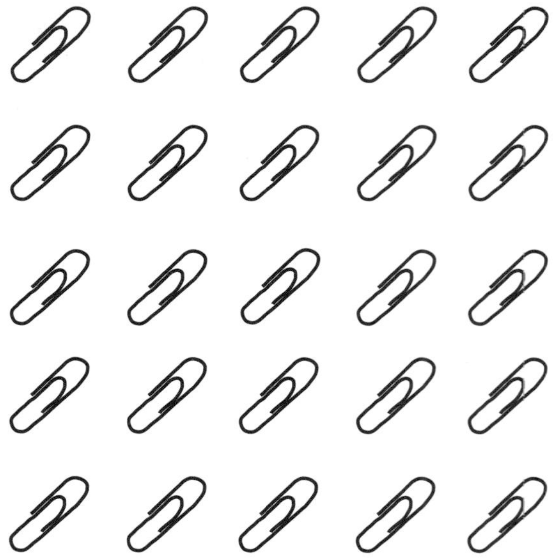

Divide the class into pairs, and provide each pair with a copy of the Game Grid and 25 paper clips, candies, or other small objects. Have the students arrange the paper clips on the Game Grid, as shown to the right.

The first player now removes either one or two paper clips from the grid. The goal of the game is to be the person who takes the last remaining paper clip, so the students must decide on the best number of paper clips to pick up on each turn. After the first player chooses either one or two paper clips, the second player then selects one or two paper clips. The game continues until one paper clip is left – the person who picks it up on their turn is the winner!

To make the directions easy for the students to understand, begin by drawing the Game Grid on the chalkboard or overhead. Choose one student with whom to play and walk through the game while the class watches.

The Gigglemaster

MATERIALS: None

DIRECTIONS:

Divide the class into pairs. Each student sits facing his or her partner. The goal of the game is for the students to try to make their partners laugh. This can be done by making funny faces or telling a joke, but the students cannot touch each other. The student that laughs is eliminated from the game.

The student from each pair that did not laugh is partnered with another student remaining in the game. Once again, each student's goal is to make his or her partner laugh. This continues until only one student remains, and this student is deemed "The Gigglemaster"!

Gone Fishin'

MATERIALS: Game Grid (page 43)

DIRECTIONS:
Provide each student with two copies of the Game Grid. Instruct each student to write the letters A-E below the bottom row of each grid, and the numbers 1-5 up the left column. Now have the students choose four different squares on one of their Game Grids. In these squares, they are to draw a picture of a fish. This grid represents the student's "pond."

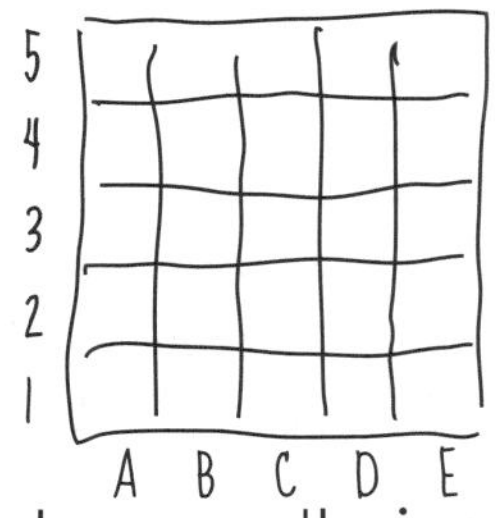

Divide the class into pairs. Tell the students not to let their partner see their pond. Have the pairs sit across from each other with the blank grids laid out in front of them. The first player begins by "going fishing" and announcing a box, saying for example, *"Do you have any fish in B-3?"* The second player secretly checks that box in their pond to see if it holds a fish. If it does, the player says, *"You caught one!"* and the first player marks an X on their blank grid in that box. If there is no fish, the second player says, *"No bites today!"* Now the players switch roles. The first player to find all four of their partner's fish is the winner!

To make the directions easy for the students to understand, begin by drawing the Game Grid on the chalkboard or overhead. Choose one student with whom to play and walk through the game while the class watches.

What's the Order?

MATERIALS: None

DIRECTIONS:
Divide the class into groups of 4-6 students. Select one group to begin the game, and have the students in the group line up next to each other at the front of the room. Give the rest of the class a few seconds to study the order in which the group has lined up.

Now have the selected group go out into the hallway and rearrange the order in which they are standing. When the group is ready, bring them back into the classroom. Have the rest of the students try to put the group back in its original order using directional vocabulary words such as "left," "right," "first," "last," etc. Encourage the students to raise their hands, and select one student to give a direction:

"Jimmy needs to move to the left of Brian."
"Rachel should be the last person in line."

After the correct order has been restored, allow one member of the first group to choose the next group to line up.

EXTENSION ACTIVITY:
Assign each group a word with the same number of letters as there are students. Have each student draw one letter from the word on a piece of paper. When it is the group's turn, the students should line up in front of the class with their letters so that the word is spelled correctly. The group can then go in the hallway, rearrange themselves, and come back into the classroom in a different order. Challenge the rest of the class to rearrange the students to spell the word correctly using directional vocabulary.

Lung Power

MATERIALS: Masking tape
Small, lightweight object (ping-pong ball, balloon, feather, etc.)

DIRECTIONS:
Clear plenty of space on the floor in the classroom. Divide the class into groups of at least four students, and distribute the groups in various places in the room. In each group's area, mark the ground with two long strips of masking tape 3-4 feet apart from each other (it may be beneficial to do this before class begins). Divide each group into two smaller groups, and have each small group kneel down behind one of the tape strips. Place a ping-pong ball, small balloon or other lightweight object within the tape strips.

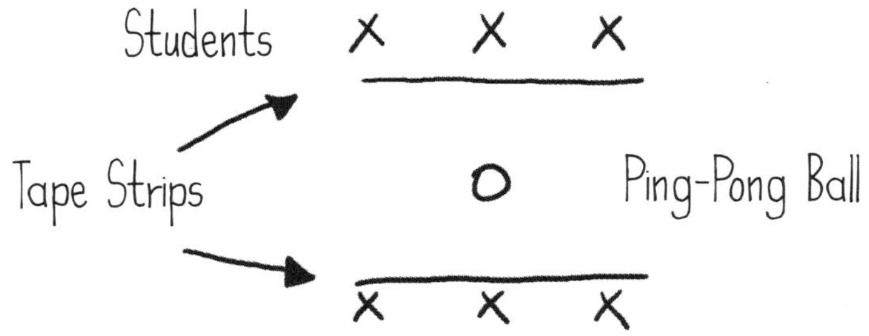

Signal the players to start blowing the items across the other team's "goal line." Players cannot at any time use their hands or cross the goal line with their knees. When a "goal" is scored, place the object back within the tape strips. The side scoring the most goals in five minutes is the winner. This game may also be played with the entire class in two groups.

Copycats

MATERIALS: None

DIRECTIONS:
Divide the class into pairs, and select one student to be the "cat" and the other the "copycat." Have the students face each other. The "cat" begins the game by moving his or her body slowly around in various ways, and the "copycat" must mirror the cat's action exactly.

The goal of the cat is to make the copycat make a mistake by making unpredictable movements or by changing the speed in which he or she moves. After one minute, the two players switch roles and begin the game again.

Around We Go

MATERIALS: Radio or CD player

DIRECTIONS:
For this activity, you will need a radio, CD player, or some kind of music source. Before beginning the activity, talk to the students about meeting new people. What kinds of questions would you ask when you meet a new person? Some suggested questions to get them started are listed below.

Divide the class in half and have each half form two circles, with one inside the other. Practice having the students in each circle walk around in opposite directions without music before beginning the activity.

Begin the music and have the circles start walking in opposite directions. When the music stops, have everybody ask the person across from him or her in the other circle a question as if they were meeting for the first time. Give the students a minute or two to answer the question, and then begin the music again.

Continue in this way for several minutes, allowing the students to practice asking and answering different questions about themselves. Students may find out things they have in common with each other that they didn't know before!

SUGGESTED QUESTIONS:
- *Do you have any brothers or sisters?*
- *What is your favorite subject in school?*
- *Do you have any pets?*
- *What did you do this weekend?*
- *What is your favorite television show?*
- *How do you get to school?*
- *What kind of music do you like?*

We Go Together

MATERIALS: Animal Cards (page 44)

DIRECTIONS:
Make enough copies of the animal cards so that each student in your class will get one card. Mix up the cards and pass out one to each student. The object of the game is for the students to group themselves together according to the pictures on their cards. Announce the groups that they are to form (suggested groups are listed below). When everyone has found a place, ask the students in each group to name the animals on their cards.

SUGGESTED GROUPINGS:
- Live on land/Live in water
- Can fly/Can't fly
- Have fur/Do not have fur
- Pets/Wild animals/Both
- Habitat (students decide specific groups—farm, zoo, ocean, etc.)

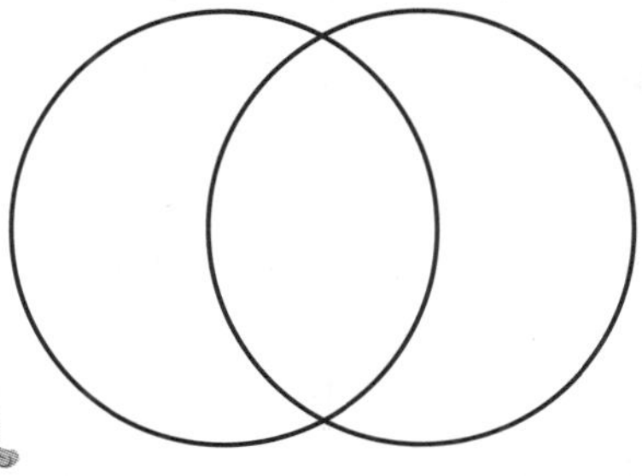

EXTENSION ACTIVITY:
Use this activity to help introduce the concept of Venn diagrams to your students. Place several pairs of hula-hoops or taped circles on the floor in the pattern of a simple Venn diagram. Designate each hoop as a particular category, and have the students physically form the Venn diagrams by separating into the hoops according to the cards.

What Do You See?

MATERIALS: Scenes (pages 41-42)
Paper
Writing Utensils

DIRECTIONS:
Divide the class into small groups. Make enough copies of one of the scenes so that each group has their own copy. The two scenes on each page are slightly different from each other, and each scene can be used for this game. Give the groups one minute to study the picture, and then take the pictures away. Give the groups two minutes to write down (or draw) all the items they can remember from the picture. The group that has the most items listed is the winner.

You may wish to use more than one picture during each game to increase the level of difficulty. For a greater variety of scenes to use, check out old magazines and catalogs.

Memory Game

MATERIALS: Common classroom objects
Sheet or cloth
Paper
Writing utensils

DIRECTIONS:
Collect 25-30 items from around the classroom (examples are listed below). Place the objects on a table or desk, and cover them with a sheet or tablecloth. Divide the class into pairs, and have everyone gather around the table. Remove the cover and give all students one minute to look at the items. After time is up, cover the items.

Provide the student pairs with a piece of paper and a writing utensil. The pairs must work together to remember as many items as possible from the table and write them on their paper.

Give the students two minutes (or an appropriate amount of time) to complete their lists. The students who can remember the most items at the end of the two minutes are the winners!

Gradually increase the number of items to be remembered to 10, 15, 20, or even 30 to challenge the students.

SUGGESTED ITEMS:
Chalk, stapler, book, worksheet, paper clips, rubber bands, school memorabilia, colored pencils, crafting supplies, bulletin board items, flashcards, stickers, hall pass

Classmate B-I-N-G-O

MATERIALS: Game Grid (page 43)
Writing utensils

DIRECTIONS:
Reproduce one copy of the grid, and fill the center of each square with an academic skill from a recent lesson or subject in class (examples are listed in the box to the right). Be sure to leave the bottom line in each square blank. Reproduce enough completed grids for each student, and pass them out to the class. The object of the game is for the students to collect one signature of a classmate that can complete that skill in each square.

For example:

Can count by 2s from 2-10 Bradley	**Can name one continent** ________
Can name two animals that live in the ocean ________	**Can name the tenth letter of the alphabet** Jennifer

Allow the students to have plenty of time to mingle and find classmates to sign their grid. The students do not need to fill up the entire grid, just enough to make a vertical, horizontal, or diagonal line. Show the students an example of each of these grids so they can see what they are trying to achieve. The first student to get enough names is the winner! Make yourself available to answer any of the students' questions
(*"Is this answer correct?", "Do I have enough signatures?"*)

Something's Different...

MATERIALS: None

DIRECTIONS:
Divide the class into pairs and have the partners stand facing each other. Allow the students to spend one minute studying each other's overall appearance; their clothes, hair, shoes, etc. After the minute, have the students turn away from each other and make a small change to their appearance, such as unbuttoning a button, rolling up a sleeve, or taking off a piece of jewelry. After everyone is ready, tell the students to turn and face each other. Challenge the students to take turns figuring out what each person changed.

The Compliment Game

MATERIALS: Object to be tossed or rolled (ball, stuffed animal, etc.)

DIRECTIONS:
Have your students sit together in a circle and provide them with a ball, stuffed animal, or other object that is safe to toss or roll between each other. The student holding the ball selects another student in the circle, tosses or rolls the ball, and gives the receiver a compliment.

Tell the students that the ball can only be tossed to a student once during each round so that everyone receives a compliment. This game helps students learn the names of the other students, and allows them to practice being polite and saying "thank you." Compliments make everyone feel good and are a great self-confidence booster.

FOR EXAMPLE:
Michelle tosses the ball to Henry.
Michelle says, *"Henry, I really like that you are always so nice to me in class."*
Henry says, *"Thank you, Michelle."*
Henry tosses the ball to Sam.
Henry says, *"Sam, you are a very good baseball player."*
Sam says, *"Thank you, Henry."*
Etc.

Partner Up

MATERIALS: Animal Cards (page 44)

DIRECTIONS:
Make enough copies of the Animal Cards so that half of the students in the class each have a different animal. Make a second set identical to the first. Put the cards in a bag or box and have each student draw a card.

The goal of the game is for each student to find his or her animal partner. Give the students a few minutes to think about their animal. Does it walk slowly or quickly? Does it walk on all four legs?

What sounds does it make?
Encourage all students to begin acting like the animal on their card at the same time. A student with a dog card may choose to bark at other classmates, while a student with a lion card may paw at their mane and ROAR! The students must find the other student that has the same card by watching their actions. Once they have found their partners, the students should stand together until the game has finished.

Mystery Foods

MATERIALS: A small variety of foods with distinct smells or tastes, such as chocolate, peanut butter, oranges, bananas, cheese, flavored snack chips, etc. Napkins, Bandannas or other blindfolds (optional)

DIRECTIONS:
This activity helps students understand the importance of two of their five senses: taste and smell. Be sure to check that students don't have any food allergies before playing this game! Prior to class, cut each food into small pieces. Divide the students into pairs, and assign one student of the pair to be TASTE and the other to be SMELL. Place a napkin in front of each pair. Blindfold all students, or have them close their eyes if blindfolds are not available.

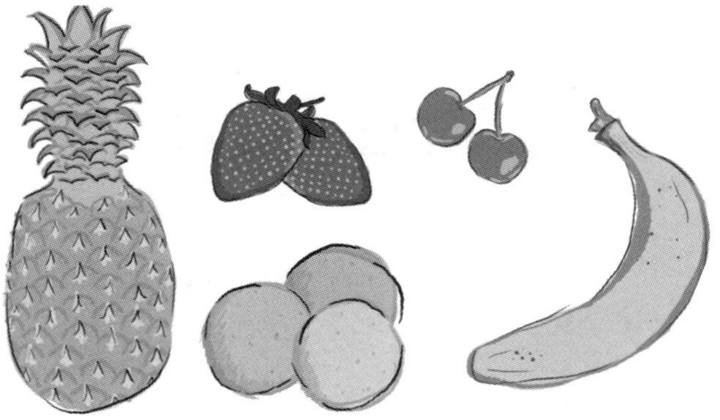

Place two pieces of the first food on each pair's napkin. Instruct all TASTE students to pick up one piece of the food and eat it (or take a bite of it). Be available to help students find the foods on their napkins. The student then describes the food to his or her blindfolded partner. Then instruct all SMELL students to pick up the other piece of food, smell it, and describe it to their partner:

SMELL partner: *What does it taste like?*
TASTE partner: *It's very fruity and sweet. It is also juicy, and kind of cold.*
TASTE partner: *What does it smell like?*
SMELL partner: *It reminds me of my favorite kind of candy, orange gummy bears.*

The goal is for the student pairs to work together to figure out the identity of the mystery food. After they have guessed, students may remove their blindfolds to see if they were correct. Continue in this way with the next food sample.

EXTENSION ACTIVITY:
Relate each food to proper nutrition and a balanced diet. To which food group does each item belong? When would this food normally be eaten? Where does it come from or how is the food made?

Hidden Messages

MATERIALS: None

DIRECTIONS:
Divide the class into small groups of 4-5 students, and have everyone sit in line with one person behind the other. The person at the end of the line "writes" a pattern on the back of the person in front of him or her (examples are given below). After the message has been written, the second person now writes the message on the back of the person in front of him or her, and so on.

After the message has reached the first person in line, check to see if it stayed the same after being written on the backs of each group member. Now have the person in the front move to the end of the line and begin a new message.

SUGGESTED MESSAGES:
- Geometric shapes
- Letters of the alphabet
- Numbers
- Short words

ABC Scavenger Hunt

MATERIALS: Lined notebook paper
Writing utensils

DIRECTIONS:
Divide the class into pairs, and provide each pair with a piece of notebook paper and a writing utensil. Have one member of each pair write the letters of the alphabet down the left-hand side of the paper. The object of the game is to find one item in the classroom for each letter of the alphabet.

The students may write or draw the answers if they wish, or they can verbally name an item and cross its first letter off the list. Students have the freedom to be as creative as they wish with their answers, as long as they find one item for each letter.

FOR EXAMPLE:

M Math book
N Nickels from my pocket
O Orange crayon

The letters Q, X, and Z can be difficult for the students to find, but you may want to leave them in to see what kind of responses the students provide!

Twists and Turns

MATERIALS: None

DIRECTIONS:
Select a few students to first demonstrate this activity to the class.

Divide the class into groups of 4-5 members, and have each group stand in a circle. Everyone should join right hands with another member of their group, but not the person next to them. Then everyone should join left hands with a different group member, but again, not the person next to them.

Each group must now untangle themselves as much as possible without letting go of each other's hands. It is important that the students in each group remain calm, work together, and avoid any roughhousing. The first group to untangle their "human knot" is the winner!

My Many Hats

MATERIALS: Many Hats Cards (pages 45-46)
Any of the following: Newspaper
12 x 21" sheet of wrapping paper
12 x 21" sheet of butcher paper
Paper grocery bags

DIRECTIONS:
Make enough copies of the Many Hats Cards so that each student will have one card. Begin the activity by helping every student create a paper hat. Directions for making a simple hat are found on page 16.

Select a few students to help demonstrate the activity before beginning with the rest of the class. To play, place a card in the brim of each student's hat so that it is easily seen by the rest of the class. Do not let the students see their own card. Divide the class into small groups of 3-4 students. Tell the students that the category of the card set is "Things Found on a Farm."

The object of the activity is for each student to identify the card in his or her hat by asking questions. Each student must ask a classmate a 'yes' or 'no' question about the card. This can be a simple question of color ("*Am I purple?*") or size ("*Am I smaller than a basketball?*"). Each question must have a 'yes' or 'no' response.

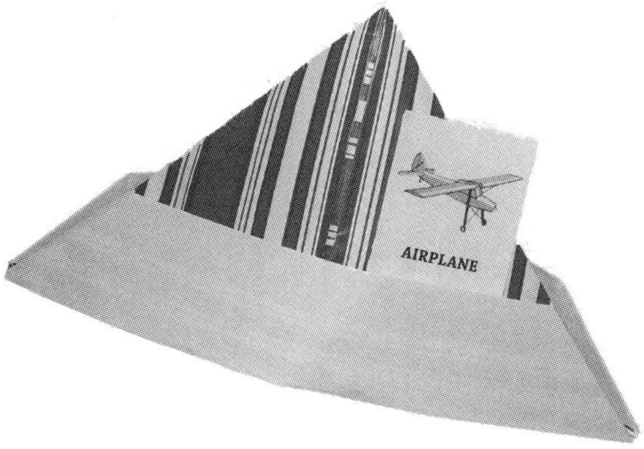

FOR EXAMPLE:
Category—Things Found on a Farm

John (corn): *Do I grow out of the ground?*
Peter (sheep): *Yes. Am I a living thing?*
John (corn): *Yes.*

Students then move on to another classmate.

Once the students believe they know the identity of their card, they may ask a student in their group to confirm ("*Am I a pumpkin?*"). This game can easily be repeated by mixing up the cards and redistributing them.

Multiple card sets, alternative hat styles, and follow-up activities are available in *Many Hats* (90/1029LE), Lorenz Educational Press, 2009.

THE HAT

These hats are very easy to make and can be used over and over again. Provide the students with markers, crayons, and colored pencils to decorate their hats before beginning the activities. This helps the student become more involved and allows them to show a bit of their creative side!

FOLDING DIRECTIONS:

1. Fold a single sheet (1 page) of newspaper (or other suggested material) in half. Fold the top corners to the center of the paper, as shown.

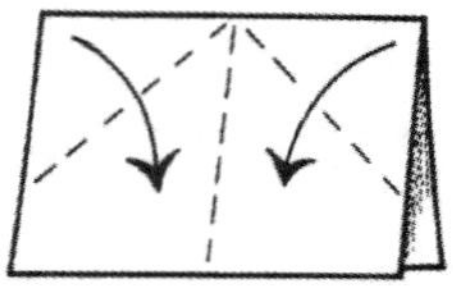

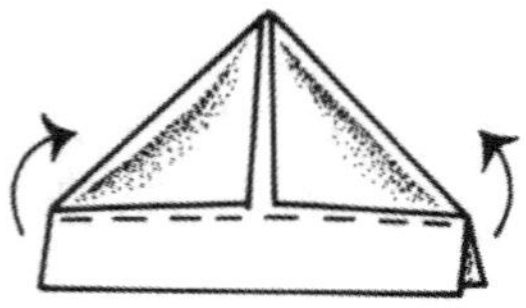

2. Fold up the bottom edge of the paper so that it is even with the bottom of the triangles. Fold the bottom edge up again to form the brim of the hat.

3. Tuck in the corners on both sides of the hat. If the hat is too small to stay comfortably on a student's head, you can punch a hole in each side of the hat's brim and tie a piece of string in each hole. These strings can then be tied under the student's chin.Another option is to use a full sheet of newspaper (2 pages), cut 4-5 inches off of the bottom, and follow the directions above. This will make a bigger newspaper hat.

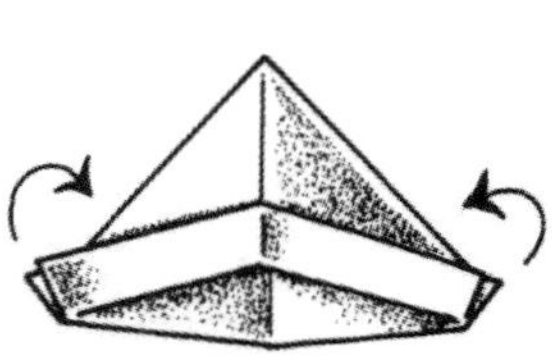

Activities to Inspire Creativity

Bring out the artistic side of your students with the activities in this section. Drawing, listening to music, acting, and other creative outlets are utilized to help your students bond with each other through the power of their own imaginations!

Illustrated Tongue Twisters

MATERIALS: Tongue Twister Cards (page 47)
Paper
Markers, crayons, or colored pencils

DIRECTIONS:
Before class begins, decide how you will divide the class into groups. Make enough copies of the Tongue Twister cards so that each group receives one card. Before beginning the activity, orally review all of the tongue twisters. Encourage the students to practice saying them aloud.

Give each group a Tongue Twister card and provide each student with a piece of paper and drawing materials, such as crayons or markers. Give the groups five minutes to draw on their papers how they visualize the tongue twister.

The groups must work together to come up with their drawings—they can all draw the same scene or different aspects of the tongue twister.

After the groups have finished, let each share their drawings with the rest of the class. Have the group say their tongue twister, and let the rest of the class attempt to say it with them. You may want to repeat the tongue twister for them a few times, as this could get confusing (and funny) very quickly!

What's Cooking?

MATERIALS: Grocery ads from the newspaper
Various old magazines
Construction paper
Glue

DIRECTIONS:
Divide the students into small groups, and provide each group with several old magazines and newspaper ads. To speed up the activity, pull out food-themed advertisements and articles from the magazines before class begins.

Challenge each group to "prepare" a dinner for the rest of the class by browsing through the magazines and cutting out the pictures of the food they would like to serve. Give each group a paper plate or piece of construction paper on which to glue their pictures. After the groups have finished, ask one group member to explain the meal they chose to the rest of the class.

EXTENSION ACTIVITY:
Talk about proper nutrition with the students. Identify the foods found on each plate and discuss in which food groups they belong. What is missing from a balanced meal? Invite the students to look through the magazines and create a healthy, well-balanced meal to serve the class.

A Zoo Without Animals

MATERIALS: Animal Cards (page 44)

DIRECTIONS:
Make a copy of the animal cards, divide the class into groups and take the first group out of the room (or away from the other groups). Have one person from the group draw an animal card. After discussing amongst themselves, the group must then silently imitate the animal in front of the rest of the class. They cannot make any sounds, but encourage the students to act out all aspects of the animal. For example:

Animal Card: Lion
Group Actions: Act out a roar, lick "paws" and rub face, brush "mane" with paws, use arm to represent tail, walk on hands and knees

Have the group "perform" their animal for the rest of the class. After the animal is correctly guessed, select another group to play and repeat the process.

Scenes From a Classroom

MATERIALS: None

DIRECTIONS:
Divide the class into small groups of 3-4 students. One at a time, have each group stand before the class and whisper an activity or event for each group to act out. These events can be anything related to a current classroom lesson or something that happens often in school. You may want to provide the class with an overall subject (science, social studies, etc.) to give them a hint.

Have each group act out their event for the rest of the class without speaking. Give the class plenty of time to study the scene, allowing them to ask questions and make comments as they watch. The group that correctly guesses the event is the next to perform. After the activity, talk with the students about the classroom lesson that relates to each event.

Select a small group of students to help you demonstrate the activity to the class before beginning.

SUGGESTED ACTIVITIES:
- Planting a garden
- Doing homework
- Playing a musical instrument
- Calling someone on the phone
- Sailing on a boat
- Going to the dentist

Help Wanted

MATERIALS: Job Classified Ads
Paper
Markers, crayons, or colored pencils

DIRECTIONS:
Collect several days' worth of job classifieds and display them so that they are accessible to all students. Give the students plenty of time to read through the classifieds as best they can together, helping each other understand words and meanings. Make yourself available to answer any questions that may arise about the jobs listed (you may want to read through several of the job descriptions together).

After the students have 10-15 minutes to look through the classifieds, provide each student with a piece of paper and drawing materials. Instruct them to draw the job that they would choose from the classified ads. When everyone has finished, have the students take turns explaining the job they drew and why they chose it.

Creative Symbols

MATERIALS: Markers, crayons, or colored pencils
Large sheet of paper

DIRECTIONS:
Divide the class into groups, and provide each group with crayons, markers, or colored pencils. Post a large sheet of paper for each group at various places in the room. (You can also use the chalkboard or give each group a sheet of paper to put on the floor.) Using a large black marker, draw a symbol on each group's paper. Some symbol suggestions have been listed below, but you may wish to use symbols that are relevant to your current lessons. Draw the same symbol on every group's paper. Talk about the symbol with the students – what does it mean? When is it used?

Select a theme for each picture. This theme can be based on a current lesson or be related to the symbol itself. Give each group five minutes to draw a picture using the symbol and theme you have provided.

You may want to do a quick example drawing to help the students get started. The group can draw any picture they choose, but they must work together on the same paper. At the end of the five minutes, have each group present their picture to the rest of the class. Let the class vote on the best picture to determine the winner!

SUGGESTED SYMBOLS:
Math: addition (+), subtraction (-)
Punctuation: period (.), comma (,), exclamation point (!), question mark (?)

SUGGESTED TOPICS:
Animals, bugs, people (professions), plants, letters, numbers, books, sports, foods

UN-common Uses

MATERIALS: Common items found around the home or classroom

DIRECTIONS:
Divide the class into small groups. Select an item that is commonly found in the home or in the classroom (examples are provided below) and show it to the groups. Challenge each group to work together to think of as many uses as possible for that item.
For example:

Item	Paintbrush	Flower Vase
Possible Uses	Paint pictures	Hold flowers
	Duster	Spare change holder
	Apply makeup	Fish bowl

Give the groups a few minutes to brainstorm on the different possible uses for the item. Take turns asking each group to give a new use for the item until the ideas run out. Select the next item and continue the activity. Another option for this game is to have the groups write down all of the possible uses, and tally up the groups' totals at the end of the game.

EXAMPLE ITEMS:
Masking tape, cooking utensils, hanger, bar of soap, laundry basket, pet dish, mouse pad, socks, hairbrush, blackboard eraser, tissues, wrapping paper, clothespin, book, CD, scarf, paper cup

At the Hop

MATERIALS: Recordings of 1950's and 60's dance songs
CD player

DIRECTIONS:
Recreate a Sock Hop by playing a few songs from the early rock era (such as *The Twist* and *Jailhouse Rock*). Teach the class the Mashed Potato, the Twist, and other classic dances and have a dance contest. The students can then form small groups and create a dance about something in their daily life. For example, the School Bus could start with a walk forward (the movement of the bus) followed by the extension of the right arm (the bus's stop sign being released).

'X' Marks the Spot

MATERIALS: Small "treasures" in varying colors, such as hard candy, lollipops, wrapped chocolates, stickers
Paper
Writing utensils

DIRECTIONS:
Divide the students into small groups of equal numbers, and provide each group with a different colored "treasure". Make sure there is enough treasure for everyone in the group to have a piece. Instruct the groups to think of one place in the classroom to hide all of their treasure. Now have all of the students close their eyes. One at a time, a member from each team should hide their group's treasure somewhere in the room.

Provide each group with a piece of paper and writing utensil. They must then draw a treasure map to be used to find their hidden treasure. The maps can include different objects in the classroom as landmarks and can be as creative as the group chooses.

After each map has been completed, collect all of the papers, shuffle them, and redistribute the maps. Make sure that no group gets their own map! Encourage the students to use the maps to find the hidden treasure. Everyone that finds the treasure gets to keep the special treat!

EXTENSION ACTIVITY:
Designate each wall of the classroom as North, South, East, or West. Let each team hide their treasure and then write a set of directions leading to it using their map skills. Encourage the students to use specific directions:

To get to the treasure:
Start at the door.
Walk 5 steps east.
Walk 3 steps north.
Look in the desk.

Secret Codes

MATERIALS: Paper
Writing utensils

DIRECTIONS:
Divide the class into small groups of 2-4 students. Challenge the students in each group to create their own secret code using letters, numbers, or pictures. They should then write a very simple message to another group. Pair up two groups and let them trade coded messages. Give the students time to decipher the other teams' secret codes, and have the teams compare their answers to see how close they are to the correct message.

Before beginning the activity, provide the students with a few example codes to get them started. This activity can also be done verbally, with one team reciting a coded message to another team that has to try and figure out the answer.

EXAMPLE CODES:
Use pictures instead of words
Scramble the letters of words
Write the letters of the words backwards
Write (or say) the words of a sentence out of order

Connect the Dots

MATERIALS: Paper
Writing utensils

DIRECTIONS:

Provide each student with a piece of paper and writing utensil, and divide the class into pairs. Instruct each member of the pair to draw 15 dots randomly on their paper. These dots can be drawn anywhere, in any pattern, as long as they are all on the same piece of paper. These dots will represent stars in the sky.

Have each student pair switch papers. Instruct everyone to connect the 15 dots (stars) drawn by their partners to make a picture. This picture will represent a new constellation in the sky. The dots can be connected with as many different lines as needed, but all dots must be used. The picture can be anything the student wishes. If possible, show pictures of existing constellations to give them some ideas.

Now have the students give their drawings back to their partners. Everyone should now try to guess the new constellation drawn by his or her partner.

Draw With Your Toes!

MATERIALS: Paper
Markers, crayons, or colored pencils

DIRECTIONS:

This game is similar to "The Blind Artist" (page 24) in that it requires the students to draw in a way that they wouldn't normally try. Give each student a piece of paper and drawing materials, and divide the class into pairs.

Have the students pretend that they no longer have the use of their writing hand. They will need to "adapt" to this change to relearn how to write. Challenge each student to draw a picture of an object, but the marker or crayon must be held with something other than their normal writing hand. Students may use their opposite hand, feet, mouth, even the crook of the arm to hold the drawing utensil. This is sure to create some unusual pictures!

Have the partners exchange pictures and see if they can guess what object the other one drew. After the activity is finished, talk about animals and the ways they have adapted over time to fit their environments. Why are polar bears white? Why do giraffes have long necks?

Thanks a Million

MATERIALS: Paper
Writing utensils

DIRECTIONS:
Provide each student with a piece of paper and a writing utensil. Encourage the class to think about all of the people in their life that they are grateful for, such as parents, family members, friends, members of the community, etc. Have the students list these people on their papers.

Next to every name, have each student write one thing about that person for which he or she is thankful. For example:

Mom – her hugs
Dad – his good chocolate cake
Teacher – her fun games

Now have the students each pick one person on their list and write a short thank you note to them. This reminds students to remember the importance of saying "thank you" and gives everyone a chance to highlight the important people in their lives.

The Blind Artist

MATERIALS: Paper
Markers, crayons, or colored pencils
Bandannas or other blindfolds (optional)

DIRECTIONS:
Provide each student with a piece of paper and drawing materials, and divide the class into pairs. Blindfold students, or have them close their eyes if blindfolds are not available. Announce that they are to draw a specific "favorite" of theirs, examples of which are listed below.

Give the students several minutes to complete their drawings. They may use different colored markers or crayons if they wish, but there is only one rule – no peeking!
It is up to the students to figure out how to complete the drawing using only their hands.

After everyone has finished, have the students remove their blindfolds and trade pictures. Now the students must guess what their partner has drawn. Let each student have a few chances to guess, then let the artist explain their picture and why they chose to draw it.

SUGGESTED TOPICS:
Favorite food, animal, TV show, subject in school, sport, actor/actress, hobby, vacation spot, movie, musician, book, thing to do on a rainy day, game, item to eat at a baseball game

Meow!

MATERIALS: Animal Cards (page 44)
Paper
Writing utensils

DIRECTIONS:
Review the letters of the alphabet with the students. Divide the class into pairs, and provide each pair with a piece of paper and writing utensils.

Make a copy of the Animal Cards and stack them in a pile. Draw one card from the stack and show it to the students. Ask them to make the sound of that animal. Now encourage each pair to write out the animal sound on their paper. Have them make the sound slowly and write down every letter that they can hear.

FOR EXAMPLE:

Animal: Cat
Sound: M E O W

Animal: Bear
Sound: G R R A R (if that's the sound your bear makes!)

Work through the first card with the students to help them understand the activity. The idea behind the exercise is for students to hear a sound, think of the letter that makes that sound, and write it down. They won't necessarily form words, just the letters associated with the sounds. Some of the animals may not make well-known noises – encourage the student to be creative with the sounds they make!

Spell With Your Hands

MATERIALS: None

DIRECTIONS:
Divide the students into pairs. Have one member of each pair act as the SPELLER, with the other student being the READER. The SPELLER must choose a letter of the alphabet and create that letter with their hands. The READER must guess the letter being created by the SPELLER. Once the letter is guessed, have the students switch roles. This allows the students to become familiar with the letters of the alphabet by having to physically create them in a way other than writing.

As the students become comfortable with the activity, the SPELLER can create short words with their hands one letter at a time. Have the READER try to figure out the word that is being spelled. You may wish to provide a vocabulary list for the students to use.

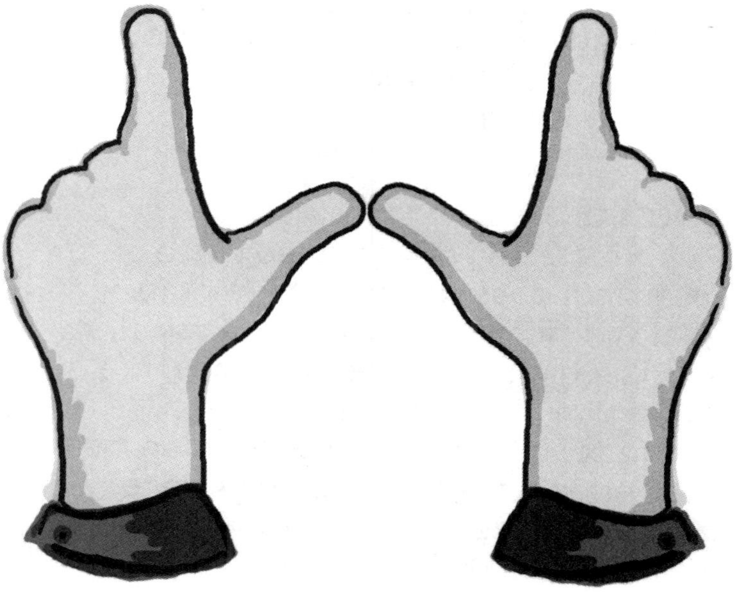

Costume Ball

MATERIALS: Newspaper
Tape
Decoration (optional):
Markers, stickers, feathers,
tissue paper, etc.

DIRECTIONS:
Divide the class into small groups, and provide each group with several sheets of newspaper and plenty of tape. The object of the game is for each group to dress one of their members in a costume made entirely of newspaper. A few costume ideas are listed below. This costume can be made to fit a specific classroom lesson, such as professions, people in history, or even animals.

Have the groups select a student to model the costume as they begin planning their design. The costume can have any theme, and the group can use as much or as little of their newspaper as they'd prefer. The costume can be taped directly onto the model to help it stay in place.

After all groups have finished creating their costumes, let the models display the finished product to the rest of the class. You may want to encourage the models to act as if he or she is in the character of the costume. Encourage the other students try to identify each costume as it is shown.

SUGGESTED COSTUMES:
Knight, mummy, robot, king/queen, hula dancer, wizard, clown, Statue of Liberty, chef

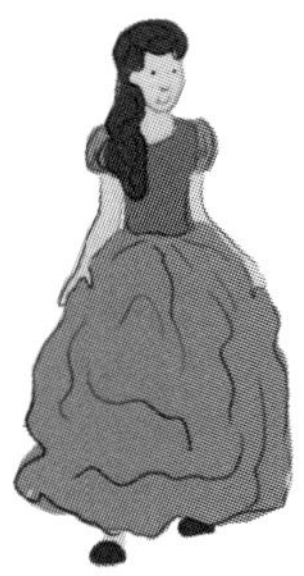

Draw the Music

MATERIALS: Music recordings of various styles
CD player
Paper
Markers, crayons, or colored pencils

DIRECTIONS:
Play a recording of a selected piece of music that does not have any lyrics (or lyrics in a different language). Classical, jazz, bluegrass, new age, and opera are all great music styles to choose from, and many free clips can be found on the internet. Feel free to choose any piece of music, but do not tell your students the name of the chosen piece. Play the recording for your students. As the music plays, challenge the students to sit quietly and listen to it carefully.

Provide each student with a piece of paper and drawing materials. As they listen through the music a second time, have the students draw the picture that the music creates in their minds. What do they think of when they hear the music? Does the music remind them of a certain time or place? Have each student present their drawing and explain it to the class. At the end of the activity, tell the students the name of the selected music.

Self-Portraits

MATERIALS: Paper
Markers, crayons, or colored pencils

DIRECTIONS:
Provide each student with paper and drawing materials. Tell the students to draw their own self-portrait. This portrait can be of just the face or could include the entire body, but the drawing should show what the student thinks they look like today. Encourage the students to talk about their drawings while they work.

After everyone has finished, collect the portraits. Show the drawings to the class one at a time, and ask the students to guess whom the portrait depicts.

Point out specific characteristics in each drawing to help the class with their guesses. What traits do the various students in the class have in common? What is different?

Speedy Speech

MATERIALS: Tongue Twister Cards (page 47)
Paper
Writing Utensils

DIRECTIONS:
Begin by reviewing all of the Tongue Twister Cards with the class. Divide the students into small groups, and provide each group with a set of Tongue Twister Cards. Give the groups time to practice saying the tongue twisters out loud.

After they have finished, have the students from each group line up behind a desk or table as shown below. Each group should place their cards face up on the desk so all of the tongue twisters can be seen:

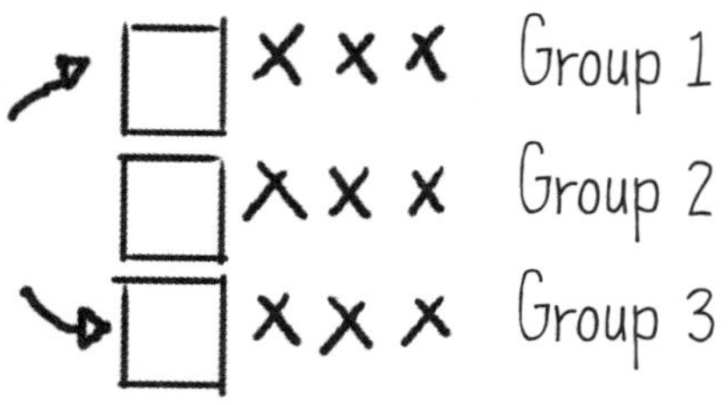

The first member in line for Group 1 picks up any card on their desk and says the tongue twister as fast (and as accurately) as possible. The rest of the groups take turns finding the same card and also saying the tongue twister as fast as possible. The group that is able to say the tongue twister the fastest with the least mistakes gets a point for the group. Now the next group member in line is up to the desk, and Group 2 selects a card. The group with the most points after going through all eight cards is the winner!

You may also want to have each group make up their own tongue twister. Write these on index cards and have the groups compete with the new set of tongue twisters. Be prepared for a lot of

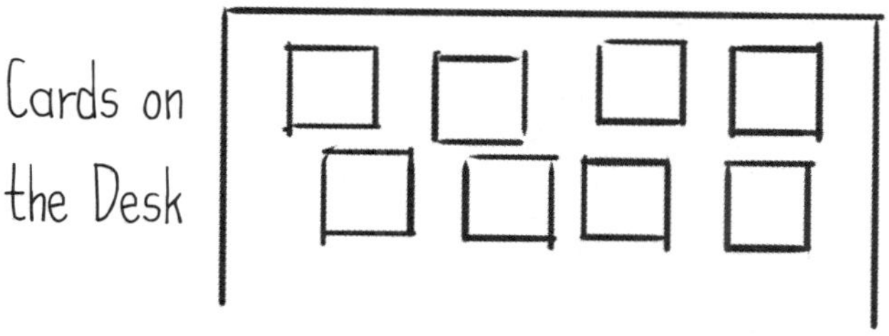

Pencil and Paper Puzzles For Pairs

These quick pencil-and-paper activities are the perfect way for your students to spend any extra minutes found in a day. Designed for use in pairs or small groups, simply photocopy the activities and let the fun begin! After they have finished the puzzles, encourage the students to color the pictures on each page.

Each activity includes instructions, but for early readers it may be beneficial to review the text together. In addition, a "How to SUDUKO!" sheet has been included for those who may not be familiar with this type of puzzle. This sheet can also be used with other types of Sudoku puzzles, which are available on the internet and at any local bookstore.

What's That Smell?

Name: ______________________ Date: ______________

You and your best friend both smell something yummy coming from the school cafeteria. But who will be the first to get to it? Place the maze between you and a partner so that each of you is next to a different table in the cafeteria. Each player enters the maze at the same time. The first player to reach the yummy treat is the winner.

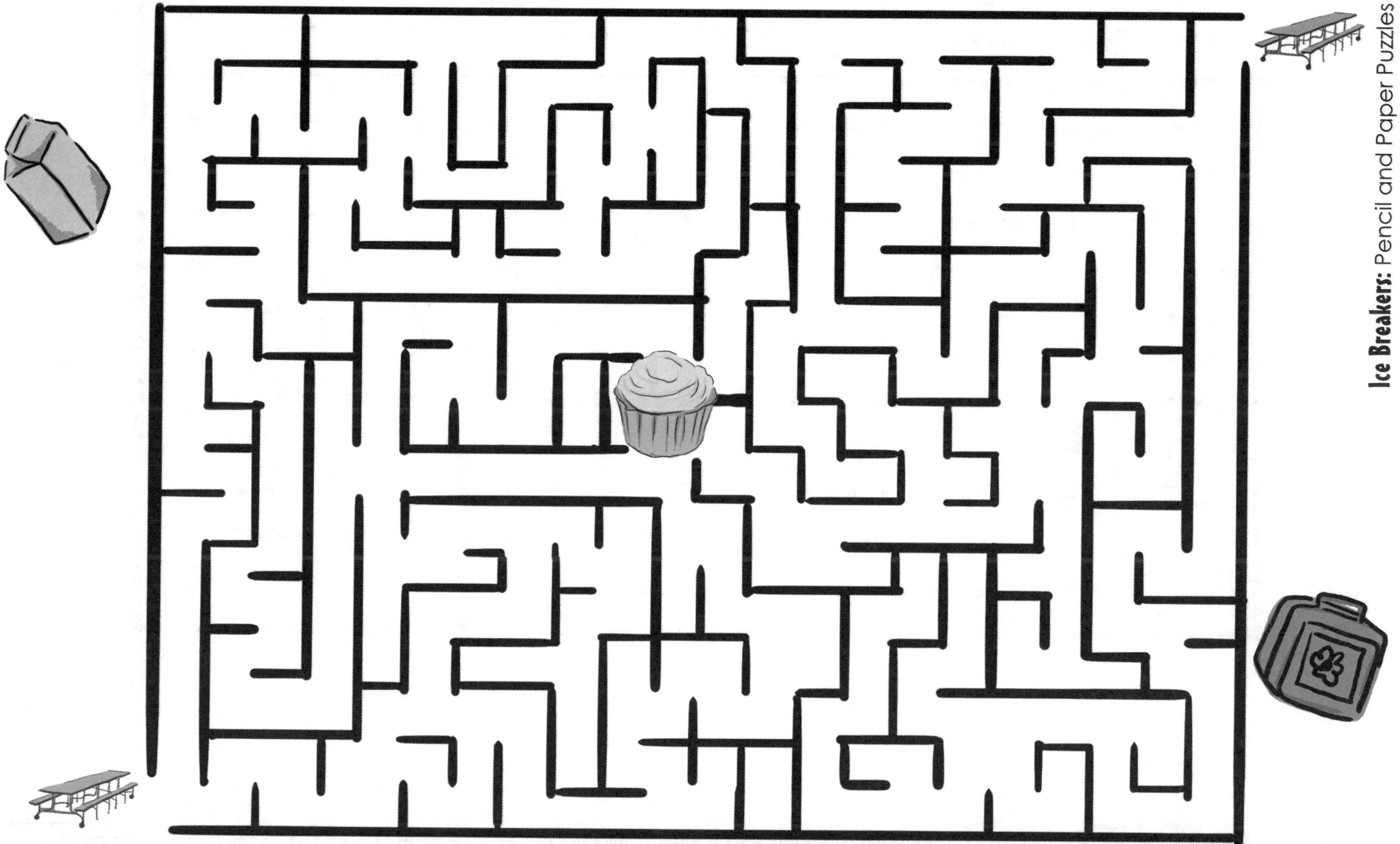

Buried Treasure

Name: ______________________________ Date: ____________________

Race against an enemy pirate to find the treasure! Grab a partner, and place the maze so that each player is behind his or her own pirate ship. Each player enters the maze at the same time. The first player to reach the buried treasure is the winner. *Avast, me hearties!*

The Case of the Missing Shoe

Name: ______________________ Date: ______________________

You and your fellow detective are competing to be the first to find Lucy's missing shoe. Place the maze between you and a partner so that you each have your magnifying glass in front of you. Begin the maze at the same time as your fellow detective, and be the first to wind your way through the house to the lost shoe!

On Your Mark, Get Set, Go!

Name: ______________________________ Date: ______________________________

Find a small group of classmates to race against in this group maze! Make sure each "runner" has his or her own copy of the maze. Have your teacher announce the start of the maze. Everyone in the race needs to begin the maze at the same time. The first player to reach the finish line is the winner. On your mark, get set… go!

How to SUDOKU!

Sudoku puzzles can be a lot of fun. You do not even have to be good at math to do these number puzzles!

The easiest kind of Sudoku puzzle is the 4x4 grid.

Here are a few things to know about doing a 4x4 Sudoku puzzle:

- Each row must have the numbers 1, 2, 3, and 4 in the boxes. Each row can only have one of each number in it.

1	3	4	2

This row has the numbers 1-4, even though they are not in order.

AND

- Each column must have the numbers 1, 2, 3, and 4 in the boxes. Each column can only have one of each number in it.

			2
			3
			1
			4

This column has the numbers 1-4, even though they are not in order.

AND

- Each small grid must have the numbers 1, 2, 3, and 4 in the boxes. Each small grid can only have one of each number in it. (You can see the small grids because they have a dark outline.)

		4	2
		1	3

This small grid has the numbers 1-4, even though they are not in order.

Put all of these rules together to fill out your Sudoku grid!
Some puzzles might be bigger than 4x4. You can still use the same rules for these puzzles.

Sometimes you might get stumped on a puzzle. To help get back on track, look for a row, column, or grid that has a lot of numbers already filled in. Look at the numbers, and see what is still missing:

3		4	2
	2		3
1			
	4	3	

The top row of this grid already has the numbers 2, 3, and 4. What's missing?

That's right – the number 1!
Fill it in, and then do it again!

Sudoku For Two – Player 1

Name: ______________________ Date: ______________________

Get a copy of "How to SUDOKU!" from your teacher. Find a partner who has a page labeled "Player 2". Work through the first puzzle as fast as you can to try and beat your partner! When both of you have finished Puzzle 1, move on to Puzzle 2.
Hint: To get started, find a line, column, or four-square box that has three of the numbers already filled in.

PUZZLE 1

1	3		
	2	1	3
	4	3	
3			2

PUZZLE 2

2	1		4
		1	2
	3	2	
1			3

Sudoku For Two – Player 2

Name: ______________________________ Date: ______________________

Get a copy of "How to SUDOKU!" from your teacher. Find a partner who has a page labeled "Player 1." Work through the first puzzle as fast as you can to try and beat your partner! When both of you have finished Puzzle 1, move on to Puzzle 2.
Hint: To get started, find a line, column, or four-square box that has three of the numbers already filled in.

PUZZLE 1

1		2	
	2	1	
2	4		1
3		4	

PUZZLE 2

	1	3	
3			2
4	3		1
1			3

Letter Sudoku

Name: ______________________ Date: ______________________

Get a copy of "How to SUDOKU!" from your teacher. Then work with your partner to fill in the six-square Sudoku grid below. In this puzzle, the letters A-F are used instead of numbers.

C	F		D	B	
	B	E		D	F
D		F	B	A	
B		C	F	E	A
E	C		A		D
	A	D	E	C	

Silly Secrets #1

Name: ______________________________ Date: ______________________________

Find a partner who has a page labeled "Silly Secrets #2." Complete the dot-to-dot puzzle below. When you are finished, fold your puzzle along the dashed line and place it next to your partner's puzzle to find the hidden message.

Where do cows go

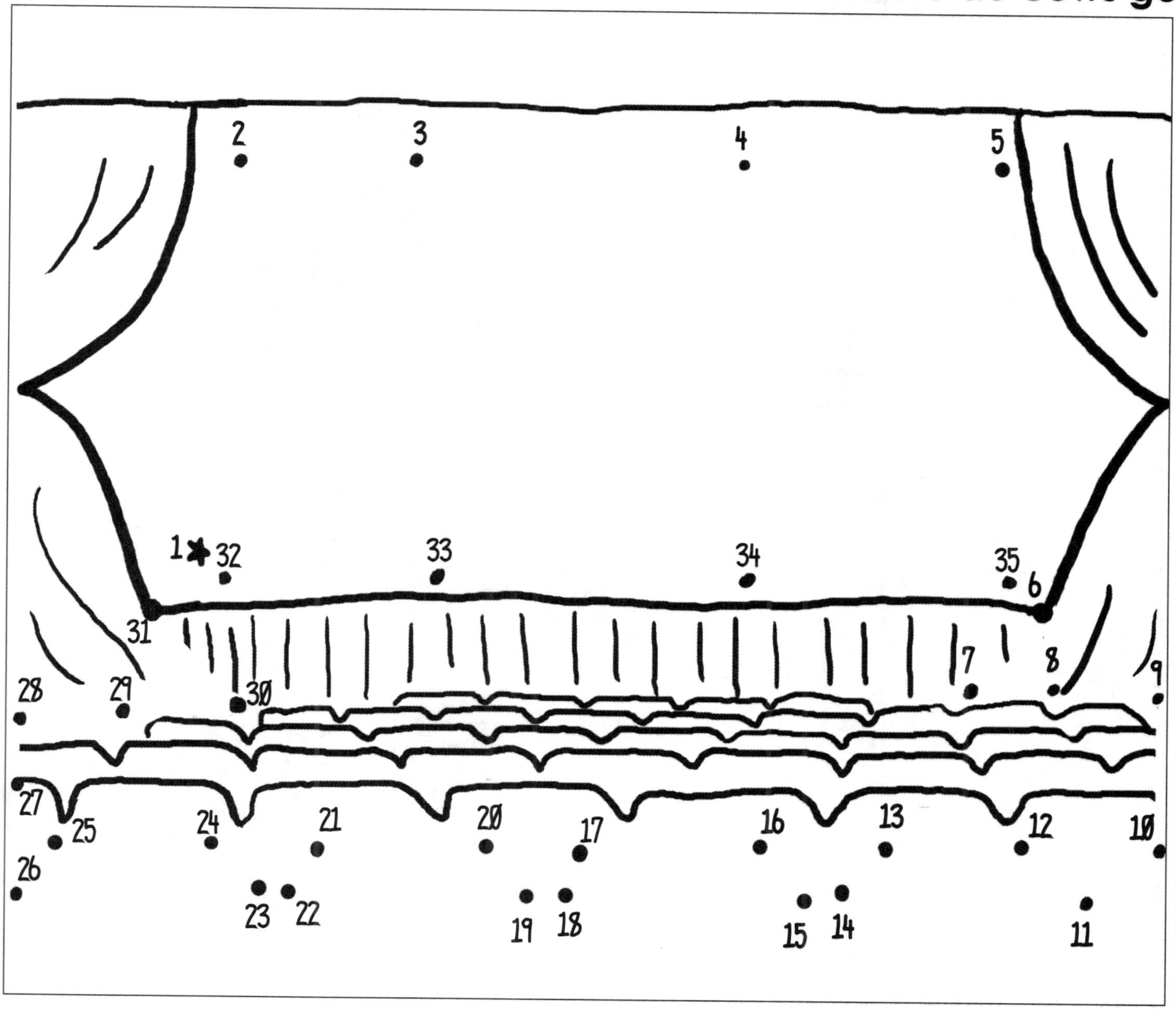

To the "Mo

Silly Secrets #2

Name: ______________________ Date: ______________________

Find a partner who has a page labeled "Silly Secrets #1." Complete the dot-to-dot puzzle below. When you are finished, fold your puzzle along the dashed line and place it next to your partner's puzzle to find the hidden message.

on Saturday nights?

o-vies!"

Puzzle Puns #1

Name: ______________________ Date: ______________________

Find a partner who has a page labeled "Puzzle Puns #2." Complete the number and letter dot-to-dot puzzles below, fold your puzzle along the dashed line and place it next to your partner's puzzle to find the hidden message.

What did one fruit say to

"Banana

Puzzle Puns #2

Name: ______________________________ Date: ______________________________

Find a partner who has a page labeled "Puzzle Puns #1." Complete the number and letter dot-to-dot puzzles below. When you are finished, fold your puzzle along the dashed line and place it next to your partner's puzzle to find the hidden message.

tease the other fruit?

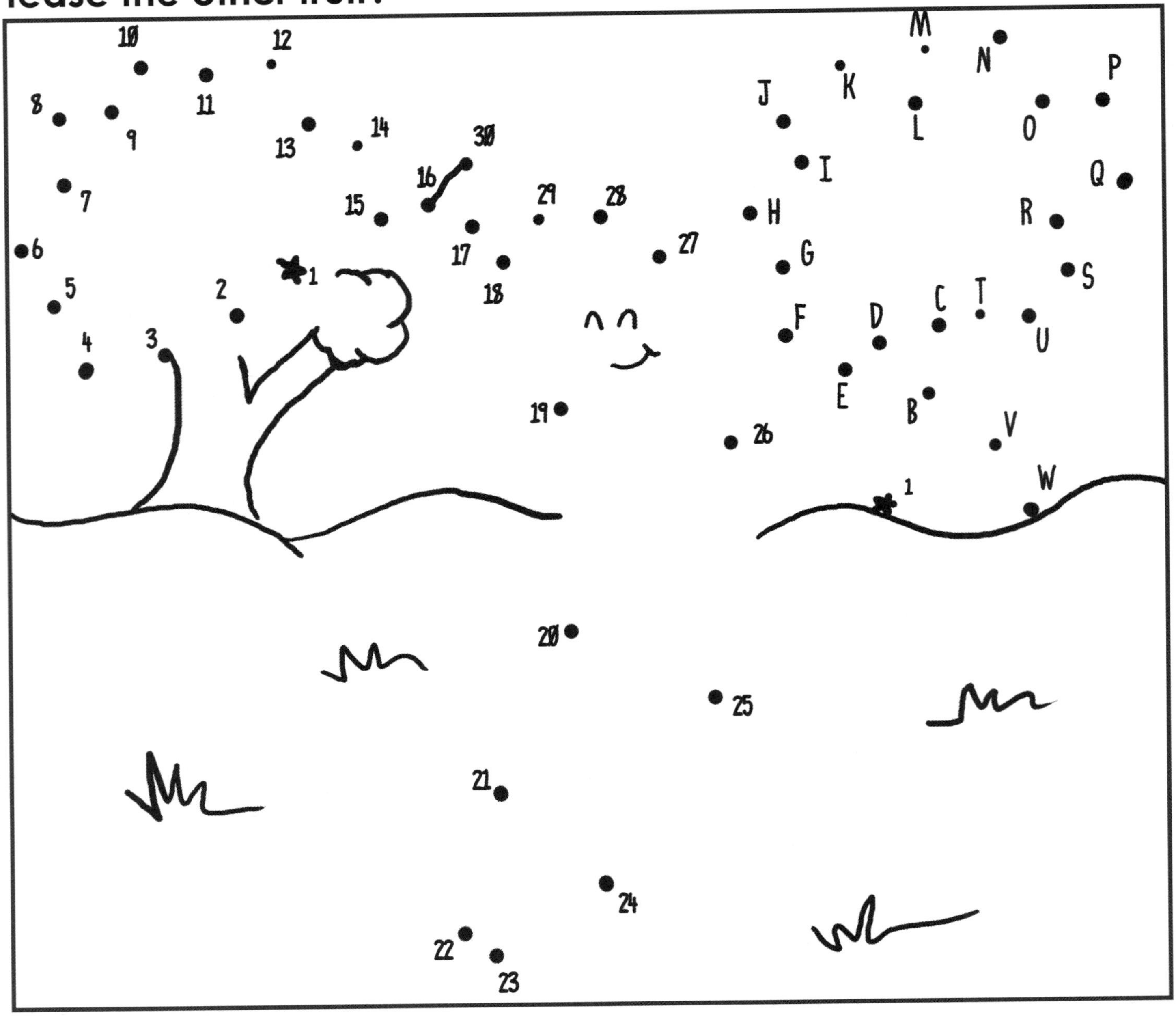

nananana!"

What's the Difference?

Name: ______________________ Date: ______________________

Look very closely at these two pictures. Work with your partner to circle everything that is not the same in both pictures.

Double Take

Name: ______________________________ Date: ______________________________

Look very closely at these two pictures. Work with your partner to circle everything that is not the same in both pictures.

DOG 	CAT 	MONKEY 	ALLIGATOR 	ELEPHANT 
GIRAFFE 	PIG 	COW 	CHICKEN 	SQUIRREL 
DOLPHIN 	BEAR 	FROG 	SNAKE 	LION 

BARN

COW

TRACTOR

PIG

SHEEP

CORN

GOAT

PUMPKIN

CHICKEN

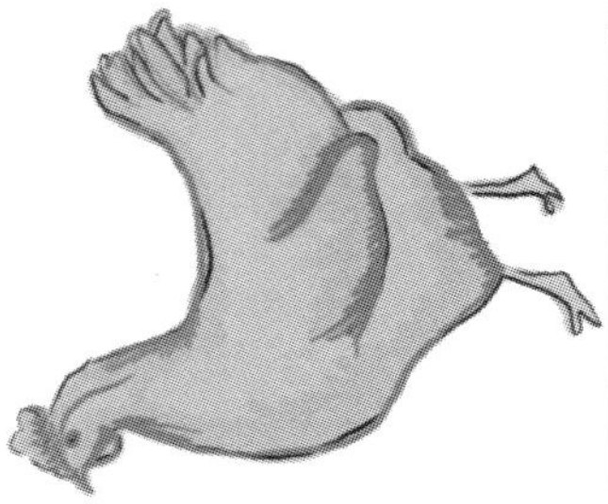

EGGS

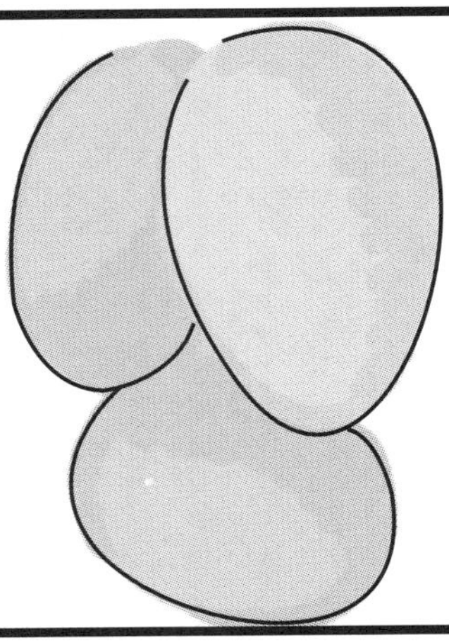

ROOSTER

HORSE

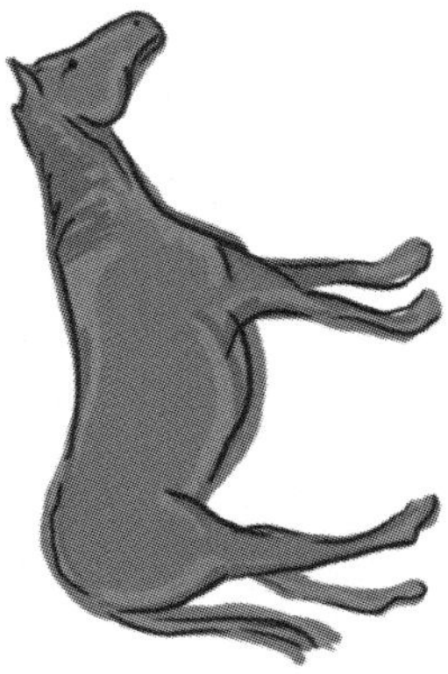

APPLE

SEEDS

CAT

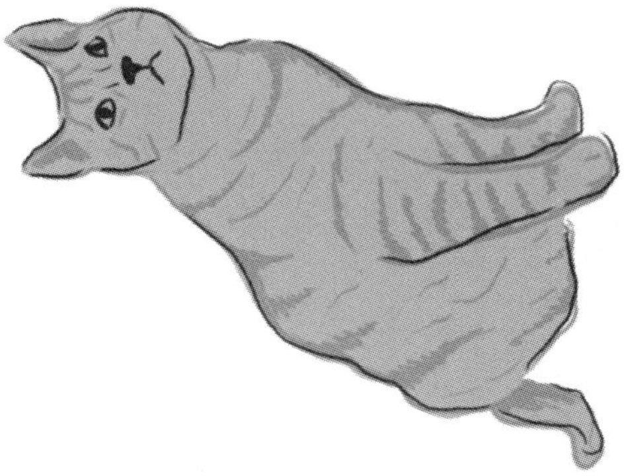

FARMER

A tricky frisky snake with sixty super scaly stripes	Peter Piper picked a peck of pickled peppers
She sells seashells by the seashore	How much wood would a woodchuck chuck if a woodchuck could chuck wood?
Betty Botter bought some butter. But, she said, "This butter's bitter. If I bought some better butter, It would make my batter better."	A skunk sat on a stump and thunk the stump stunk, but the stump thunk the skunk stunk.
If Stu chews shoes, should Stu choose the shoes he chews?	Papa wants a proper cup of coffee from a proper copper coffee pot.
Double bubble gum bubbles double	Fuzzy Wuzzy was a bear Fuzzy Wuzzy had no hair Fuzzy Wuzzy wasn't very fuzzy, was he?

Answer Key

"What's That Smell?," pg. 29

"Buried Treasure," pg. 30

"The Case of the Missing Shoe," pg. 31

"On Your Mark, Get Set, Go!" pg. 32

"Sudoku for Two," pg. 34-35

1	3	2	4
4	2	1	3
2	4	3	1
3	1	4	2

2	1	3	4
3	4	1	2
4	3	2	1
1	2	4	3

"Letter Sudoku," pg. 36

C	F	A	D	B	E
A	B	E	C	D	F
D	E	F	B	A	C
B	D	C	F	E	A
E	C	B	A	F	D
F	A	D	E	C	B

"What's the Difference?" pg. 41

1. Tree outside moved
2. Lamp moved
3. Ceiling fan
4. Bedding pattern
5. Teddy bear
6. Headboard color
7. Chair
8. Birds
9. Clock time
10. No vase

"Double Take" pg. 42

1. Missing curtain
2. Wall color
3. Rug pattern
4. Cat's tail
5. Night and day outside
6. Lamp
7. Glass filled with milk
8. Missing pillow
9. Picture frames switched
10. Missing picture